New National Curriculum Edition

INTO GEOGRAPHY

BOOK 2

Patricia Harrison   Steve Harrison   Mike Pearson

Acknowledgements

British Gas
Linda Edmondson
Ann Farshaw
Paul Gamble
James Price
Revoe C.P. School, Blackburn
St. Thomas' Church of England School, Blackburn
Thames Water Authority
The Patel family, Bharuch, India
The Ul -Haqq family, Jhelum, Pakistan
World Health Organisation

Photographs by Aerofilms p.56; DAS London p.12; Dinodia p.12;
Steve Harrison pp.13, 35, 50; Sally & Richard Greenhill p.10;
A.G.E. Fotostock p.14; Hutchison Library p.32; Image Bank p.53;
Milk Marketing Board of England and Wales p.44; Netherlands Board of
Tourism p.46; Network pp.35, 58; N.H.P.A. p.61; Picture Bank pp. 46, 53;
Q.A. Photos Ltd p.51; Tony Stone p.60; The Mining Journal Ltd p.51

Cover photograph supplied by Pictor International

Illustrated by Terry Bambrook, Ray Mutimer, John Plum, Barrie Richardson,
Colin Smithson, Taurus Graphics

Thomas Nelson and Sons Ltd
Nelson House Mayfield Road
Walton-on-Thames Surrey
KT12 5PL UK

51 York Place
Edinburgh
EH1 3JD UK

Thomas Nelson (Hong Kong) Ltd
Toppan Building 10/F
22a Westlands Road
Quarry Bay Hong Kong

Thomas Nelson Australia
102 Dodds Street
South Melbourne
Victoria 3205 Australia

Nelson Canada
1120 Birchmount Road
Scarborough Ontario
M1K 5G4 Canada

© Patricia Harrison, Steve Harrison, Mike Pearson 1986, 1992

First published by E J Arnold and Son Ltd 1986
ISBN 0-560-66712-4

Fully revised second edition published by Thomas Nelson and Sons Ltd 1993
ISBN 0-17-425052-5
NPN 9 8 7 6 5 4 3 2

Printed in Great Britain.

CONTENTS

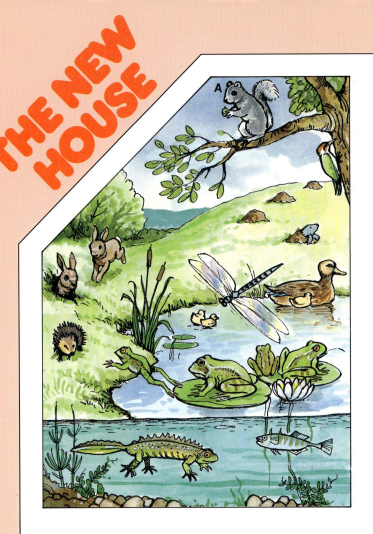

Sally and David's new house will be on a large housing estate. The builders have bought the land from a farmer. Soon they will start to build.

Sally and David visit the fields where their house will be built. This is what they see.

Assignment A

1 If you look carefully you will find ten creatures in the picture. List them.

2 Now complete the chart. Two have been done for you.

ANIMAL	UNDER-GROUND	ON THE GROUND	IN WATER	ABOVE THE GROUND
Wood-pecker				🐦
Frog		🐸	🐸	

Some builders clear the ground completely before they build new houses.

Assignment B

1 Look at picture B. Describe what has happened.
What has been destroyed?

2 Imagine you are a rabbit. One morning you hear the sound of a bulldozer. Your home will be destroyed in ten minutes, your young ones are playing in the field. Write a story called 'The earth-eating machines'.

One step further

Some builders think that the trees, hedges, and ponds will make the estate a more interesting place for people to live. Would you find it more interesting?

A

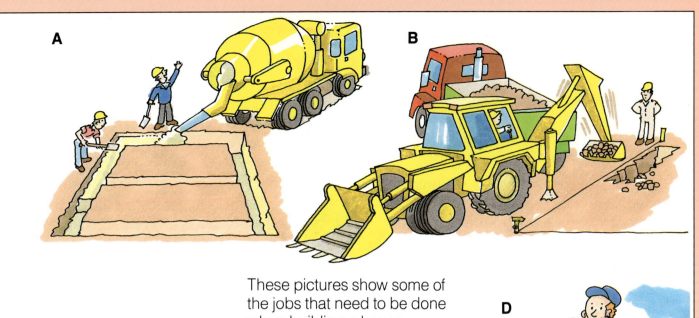

B

These pictures show some of the jobs that need to be done when building a house.

Assignment C

1 Write a sentence about each picture describing what is happening.

2 It is impossible to tile the roof before the walls are built.

Can you put the jobs shown in the pictures into the correct order?

Start like this:
First, the foundations must be dug out by an excavator.

Second, ...

C

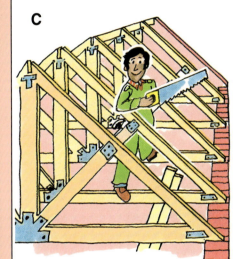

D

E

F

5

TIMBER

Sally's Uncle John works in a factory making window frames, doors and roof joists out of wood.

Most of the wood comes from British Columbia.

British Columbia is a part of a country called Canada. We don't grow enough trees in our country so we have to buy extra wood from abroad.

3   Is British Columbia on the east or the west side of Canada?

4   The ships bringing timber from British Columbia to the United Kingdom have a long journey.
Which two oceans do they sail on?
Which canal do they pass through to get from one ocean to the other?

5   How many kilometres is it by sea from Vancouver to Liverpool? Use a piece of string to measure the distance.

Assignment A

1   Look around your classroom.
Make a list of things you can see made of wood.

2   The countries 1-5 on the map sell wood to the United Kingdom.
Use your atlas to find their names.

One step further A

Use an atlas to draw a map of Canada.
Mark on British Columbia and the other provinces of Canada.
Shade each one a different colour.

Find out the main town of each province and add them to your map.

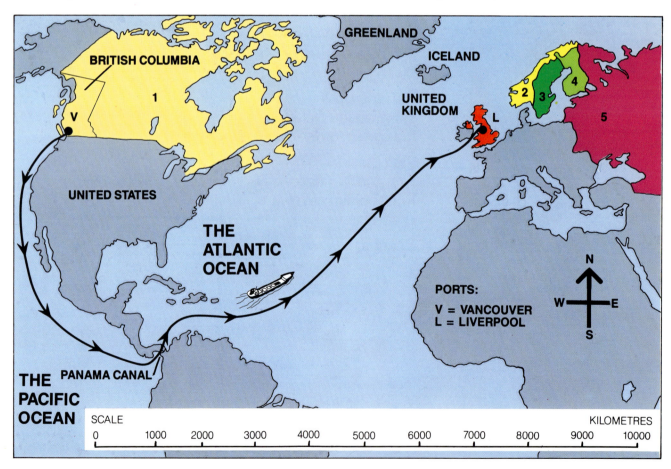

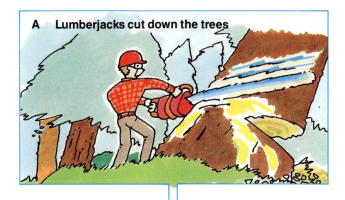

A   Lumberjacks cut down the trees

British Columbia has many coniferous trees. Coniferous means bearing cones. Most coniferous trees are evergreen, which means that they keep their needle-like leaves all the year round. One evergreen you will know is the Christmas tree. Its correct name is the Spruce tree. We grow a lot of Sitka Spruce in hilly areas of the United Kingdom. The Sitka Spruce was found originally in British Columbia and Alaska. Other coniferous trees that grow well in British Columbia and in the United Kingdom are the Douglas Fir and the Western Red Cedar.

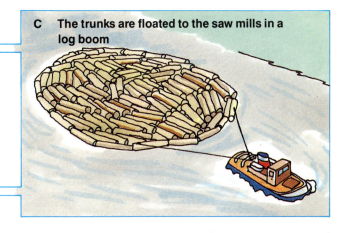

B   The tree trunks are transported to the river

C   The trunks are floated to the saw mills in a log boom

D   The trunks are sawn into planks

E   The planks are loaded onto ships in Vancouver

F   Meanwhile students as a holiday job plant young trees for the future

Assignment B

1 Describe the jobs being done in each picture.

2 What are the people who cut down trees called?

3 What are they wearing for protection?

4 How is the timber being transported in B and in C?

5 What is used to change the tree trunks into planks in the saw mill?

One step further B

What would happen if new trees were not planted?

BUILDING A HOUSE

A great deal of planning is needed before a house can be built and sold. The correct materials and services must also be provided. Mortar for the bricklayer can only be mixed if water is available on the building site. The glazier can't fit the glass until the joiner has fitted the window frames.

Look at this picture. It shows a house which has been built without planning. Make a list of all the things that are wrong.

Glazier, water company worker, advertiser, electrician, architect, bricklayer, painter, Telecom engineer.

1 Find out what each person in the list does. Write a sentence about each one, beginning like this:
An architect is someone who …

2 When you have found out what each worker does match the name of the worker with the correct picture.

Do it like this:
Picture B shows a bricklayer.

One step further

1 The water company brings water to the building site. They provide a **service**. The glaziers work on the houses so they are **on site**. The estate agent sells the house. She works in an office **off site**.

Put the occupations into the correct list.

SERVICES	ON SITE	OFF SITE

2 Which of these services do you have in your home? Gas, electricity, water, mains drains, septic tank, telephone, cable T.V.

3 Choose either electricity or water. Write about what your life would be like if you did not have it supplied to your home.

4 Apart from electricity can you list three other fuels which are used for heating homes?

Zoe used to live with her mum and dad in a small house. When dad left home they went to live with Zoe's grandparents in a one-bedroomed flat. Mum and grandma argued about the overcrowding and about mum not having money or a job.

Assignment A

1 Where do Zoe's mum and the grandparents sleep?

2 Why do you think Zoe kept falling asleep in class?

3 Can you give three reasons why Zoe isn't getting a peaceful night's sleep?

4 Why don't grandma and grandad's friends visit them very often?

Not everyone in Britain has a home. Sometimes whole families live in one small room. Today there are over 100,000 homeless families in Britain. Some do not even have a room to live in. They have no home at all.

One night Zoe's mum couldn't stand living in the flat any longer. She had heard that there might be jobs in London.

The train arrived in London early in the morning.

Zoe asked her mum whether they would have to sleep in the streets.

Zoe's mum found a job agency. They said they could not find her a job unless she had a permanent address.

Many owners refused to rent rooms to anyone with children.

Others would only rent a room to Zoe's mum if she had a job.

Late in the evening Zoe and her mum were given a bed in a hostel for the homeless. They were told it would be for one night only.

Assignment B

1 Why do some owners not want children in the rooms they rent?

2 Why will many owners only rent rooms to people with jobs?

3 Why wouldn't the job agency help Zoe's mum to find a job before she has a local address?

4 Write a story about Zoe's life in the flat and in London.

One step further

CHOICES. Zoe's mum had to make a decision. She could either

a) Put Zoe into care so that she could rent a room in London.

b) Walk the streets another day looking for work and a home, but risk having to sleep rough.

Can you think of three other choices Zoe's mum could make?

Which choice would you make? Say why.

India is a very large country. It has some of the world's highest mountains. They are covered in snow all year round. There are deserts which are hot and dry. Some parts of India have heavy rainfall. Other areas suffer from drought.

The weather affects the styles of houses. Homes in rainy areas need steep roofs to keep the rain out.

The material available for building is also important.

In forest areas the homes are often made of wood.

In farming areas it is easier to dig clay from the ground to make bricks for building.

Many people need a home that allows them to earn a living.

Some families trade on the lakes and rivers so they live in houseboats.

Assignment A

Imagine you live in a houseboat.

Write about your life.

Think about school, play, babies, friends, danger, skipping, ballgames.

This is a new house being built on the edge of a village.

Assignment B

Look carefully at the picture.

1　Is this house built in an area of high or low rainfall?

2　Why do you think the windows are small and have ledges over them?

One step further A

Compare your home with this Indian house.

Look carefully at the roof, the windows and the shape of the house.

Can you explain the differences?

This is the house of a Hindu family in another part of India. They have a downstairs, an upstairs and a loft.

It can get very hot in India.

What is used to cool the room?

This is what you see looking at the loft roof from the bed.

Assignment C

Look carefully at this picture of the loft which is used for storage.

1 What materials are used for:

a) The walls   b) The roof   c) The floor.

2 Can you tell whether this house is in a farming or forest area?

3 Do you think there is more or less rain in this area than there is where the new house has been built?

Cooking is usually done outside. Today it is raining so the cooking must be done inside.

Assignment D

1 What fuel is being used?

2 Why is the woman squatting?

One step further B

1 There are no carpets in any room. Can you say why?

2 Why is there no meat in this Hindu home?

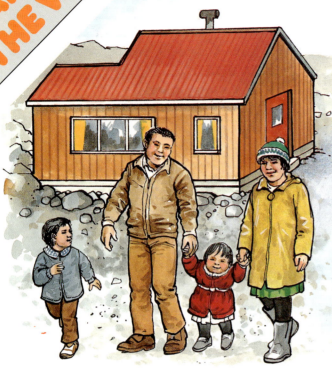

This is an Inuit house in Northern Alaska. Inuit is the Eskimo word for people. The ground is frozen for most of the year and it is too cold for trees to grow. Inuit houses have to be protected from the cold ground and cold air. This is done by putting thick plastic padding in the bottom, sides and roof of the house. We call this **insulation**.

These are traditional adobe Indian houses in Mexico. Adobe means sun dried mud bricks. Mexico is a hot country. These houses have been cleverly built to protect people from the fierce heat of the sun. Look at the thickness of the walls and the small size of the windows. The thick walls also keep the house warm at night. The weather can get very cold in the night in deserts.

Assignment A

1 Complete the table.

HOUSE	WHAT IS IT BUILT OF?	WHAT HAS IT TO BE PROTECTED FROM?	HOW IS IT PROTECTED?
Modern Inuit house			
Traditional Indian house			

2 What clue tells us there is little rain where the adobe houses are?

One step further A

1 Using an atlas find Alaska and Mexico.

2 Which is closer to the North Pole?

3 Which is closer to the Equator?

In some parts of the world the winters are much colder than in the United Kingdom (U.K.).

This is the living room of a Swedish house. Swedes usually keep their houses warmer in winter than we do.

Assignment B

1 Is it winter or summer in this Swedish house?

2 What do you wear in your home in cold winter weather?

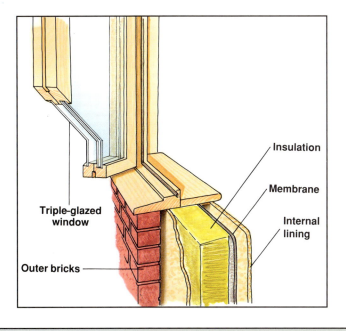

Triple-glazed window

Outer bricks

Insulation

Membrane

Internal lining

One step further B

Look at newspapers to find out what the noon time temperatures were in the cities shown in this chart. Record your findings.

1 Date ___ Month _____ Season _____

CITY	COUNTRY	TEMPERATURE (°C) AT 12 NOON
London	U.K.	
New York	U.S.A.	
Moscow	Russia	
Tokyo	Japan	

2 The average temperatures for the above cities are:

CITY	AVERAGE JANUARY TEMPERATURE (°C)	AVERAGE JULY TEMPERATURE (°C)
London	+4	+18
New York	-1	+23
Moscow	-14	+19
Tokyo	+5	+26

Which is the coldest of these places in January?

Which is the hottest of these places in July?

DOES SIZE MATTER?

Vincent Van Hire is a famous Dutch artist but he has a problem. He cannot draw objects the right size.

Assignment A

Look at the picture Vincent has painted.

1 How many things can you spot which are the wrong size?

Write a sentence about each. One is done for you.

'The man is bigger than the car'

2 Can you help Vincent Van Hire?

Draw the picture. Make everything the correct size.

One step further

Ronald was tired of being smaller than his brother. One night he sneaked downstairs and stood in the gro-bag his parents used for growing tomatoes. Every hour Ronald poured water over his head. Next morning Ronald was 4 metres tall and then life became interesting .....

Write a story about Ronald's first day as a four metre giant.

Look at the two drawings of the Church. The pictures are the same shape but the size is different.

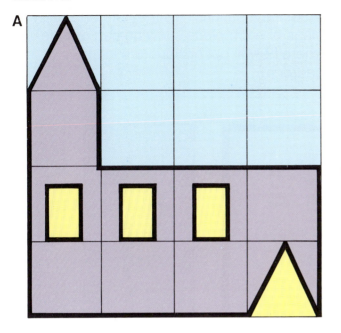

A

Using your ruler complete the chart:

	CHURCH A	CHURCH B
Height of doorway	2 cm	
Height of tower		4 cm
Width of window		
Width of doorway		
Length of church		

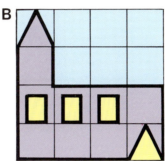

B

What do you notice about the size of Church A compared to Church B?

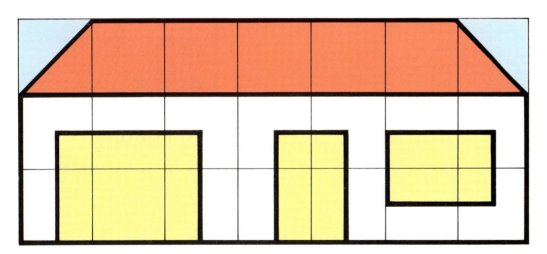

Assignment C

The picture of the house has been drawn on squares with sides 2 cm long. Copy the picture onto paper which has squares with sides 1 cm long. Your picture will then be exactly half the size of the picture in the book.

Assignment D

Measure these drawings. Remember 1 cm on the drawing stands for 1m on the real object.

How long is the car?

How high is the lamppost?

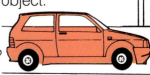

David drew a plan of his new bedroom. The bedroom is 4 metres long and 4 metres wide. He measured his furniture and drew plans of each piece. Now he can decide where he will put his furniture in the bedroom.

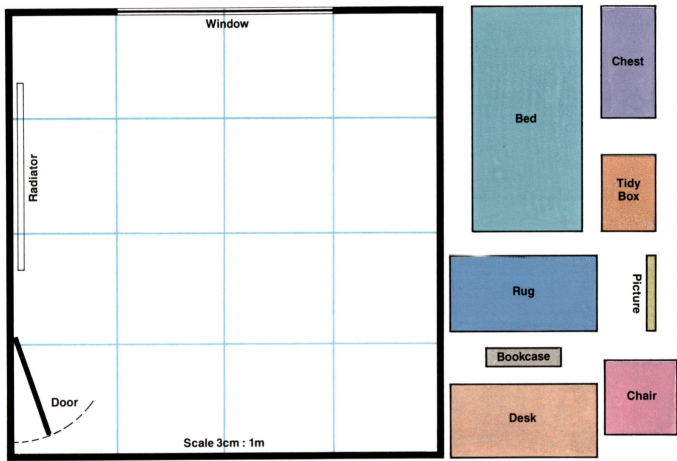

Window

Radiator

Door

Scale 3cm : 1m

Bed

Chest

Tidy Box

Rug

Picture

Bookcase

Chair

Desk

Assignment A

1 Is David's room a square or an oblong?

2 Trace or copy the plan of David's bedroom.

3 Trace and cut out the pieces of furniture.

4 Plan David's room by moving the cut-outs around.

5 When you are happy with your arrangement glue them onto the plan.

One step further

1 Draw a plan from memory of what your bedroom looks like.

2 When you go home measure your bedroom and your furniture.

3 Now draw an accurate plan of your room. Compare it with the plan you drew from memory.

Mr and Mrs Johnson have planned their new garden. The scale is 1 cm on the plan for 2 m in the garden. We write this scale as 1 cm : 2 m

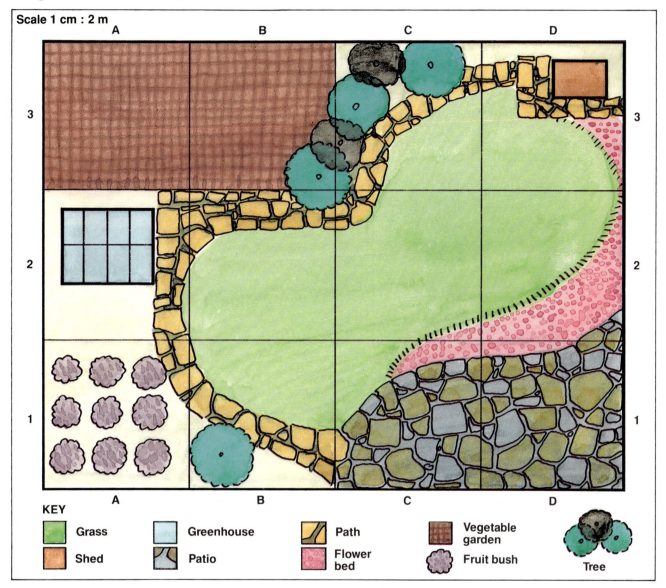

Scale 1 cm : 2 m

KEY

Grass | Greenhouse | Path | Vegetable garden | Tree
Shed | Patio | Flower bed | Fruit bush

Assignment B

1 Measure the length of the greenhouse, shed and vegetable garden and complete the chart.

LENGTH OF	ON THE PLAN	IN THE GARDEN
Greenhouse		
Shed		
Vegetable Garden		

2 Use a piece of string to measure the length of the path.

3 The shed is **located** in grid square (D,3). We call this a **grid reference**.

Write the grid reference for
a) The greenhouse b) The fruit bushes.

4 The vegetable garden is located in two grid squares (A,3) and (B,3).

5 List the grid squares in which there is grass.

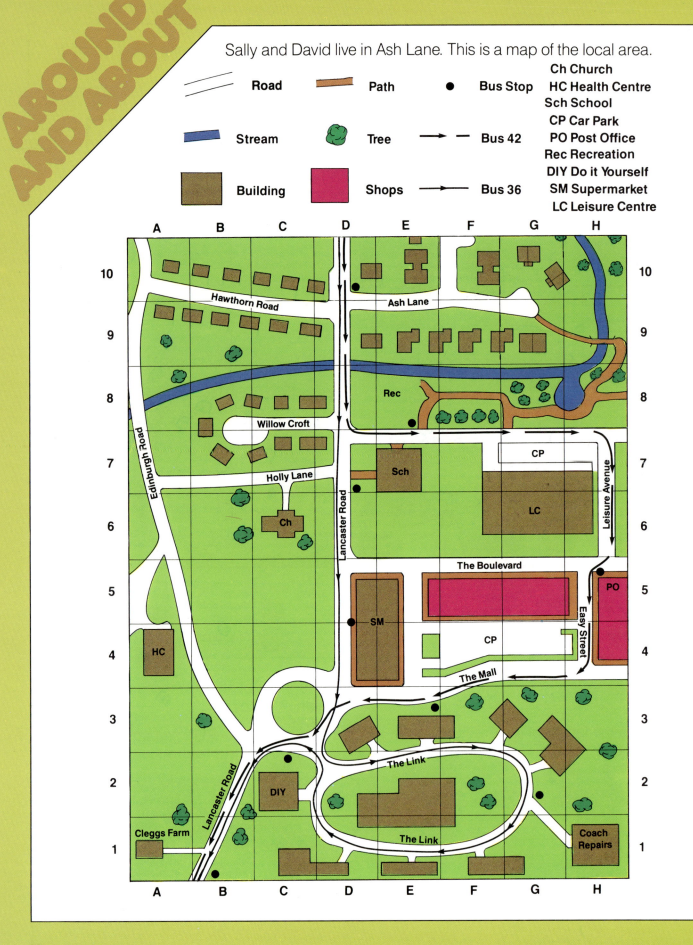

Sally and David live in Ash Lane. This is a map of the local area.

Road   Path   ● Bus Stop

Stream   Tree   →--- Bus 42

Building   Shops   →— Bus 36

Ch Church
HC Health Centre
Sch School
CP Car Park
PO Post Office
Rec Recreation
DIY Do it Yourself
SM Supermarket
LC Leisure Centre

Hawthorn Road
Ash Lane
Edinburgh Road
Willow Croft
Rec
CP
Holly Lane
Sch
Lancaster Road
LC
Ch
Leisure Avenue
The Boulevard
SM
CP
PO
HC
Easy Street
The Mall
Lancaster Road
The Link
DIY
Cleggs Farm
The Link
Coach Repairs

1   Which buildings are in the following grid squares:
    a) (E,7).   b) (C,6).   c) (A,1).   d) (A,4).

2   Give the grid references for:

    a)   The D.I.Y. Store.
    b)   The Coach Repairers.
    c)   The Post Office.

One step further A

If you caught the No. 42 bus from Ash Lane to Clegg's Farm. What would you see from the window on your right-hand side? Describe your journey.

This is the bus timetable displayed at the Ash Lane bus stop. Sally and David use it to check the times of buses.

BUS TIMETABLE

BUS NO. 42			
Ash Lane	07.30	08.30	09.30
Central School	07.32	08.32	09.32
Post Office	07.35	08.35	09.35
Supermarket	07.38	08.38	09.38
D.I.Y. Store	07.40	08.40	09.40
Clegg's Farm	07.41	08.41	09.41

BUS NO. 36		
Ash Lane	08.00	09.00
Central School	08.02	09.02
Supermarket	08.04	09.04
Coach Repairs	08.07	09.07
D.I.Y. Store	08.09	09.09
Clegg's Farm	08.10	09.10

Assignment B

1   Sally and David live in Ash Lane. They must be at the Central School before 9 o'clock.
    Which number bus should they catch?
    What time will they get on the bus?

2   Mr Johnson works at the Coach Repairers. He starts work at 08.30.
    Which number bus should he catch?
    What time does it leave Ash Lane?
    Why would Mr Johnson prefer to start work at 08.15?

3   Mrs Johnson has arranged to meet a friend at the supermarket at 09.45.
    Which bus should she catch?
    What time does it leave Ash Lane?

4   Which bus takes longer to reach Clegg's Farm, No. 36 or No. 42?
    How much longer does the journey take?

One step further B

David needs to know the times of No. 42 buses back to Ash Lane.

Complete this timetable for him. Fill in the missing names of the bus stops and the missing times. The 42 bus follows the same route as on the map but in the opposite direction.

TIMETABLE FOR NO. 42 BUS
Displayed at Clegg's Farm.

Clegg's Farm	08.04	09.04		11.04
	08.05		10.05	
Supermarket				
Post Office		09.10		
Ash Lane	08.15			11.15

PEOPLE WE NEED

In an emergency

1. Dial 999
2. Say which service you want.
3. Wait for the service to answer.
4. Give the telephone number shown on the telephone.
5. Give the address where help is needed.

A B C

D E F

1 Look carefully at the picture of Bedlam Boulevard.
Help is needed. Complete the chart.
You will need a telephone directory to find the correct numbers.

EVENT	SERVICE NEEDED	TELEPHONE NO.
House on fire	Fire Brigade	999

2 When you have found your local emergency numbers write them onto a piece of stiff card and keep it at home by the telephone.

3 Which emergency services are shown on your chart?

4 Can you name some more emergency services?
Look in the telephone directory.

G

One step further

1 Apart from catching burglars the police have many other jobs to do. List as many of these as you can.

2 Do the same for the other services shown on this page.

3 Write about what happens next in each of the events shown in Bedlam Boulevard.

4 Imagine you saw the man in the striped shirt climbing in through a window. The telephone was out of order.
What did you do?
Tell the story of how you and your friends came to the rescue.

1   If you were driving the fire engine which route would you choose from the fire station to the fire?

Describe your route. Say which roads you drive along, whether you turn right or left, and which buildings you pass.

2   A crash has taken place on Canberra Road, outside the public house. If you chose this road to reach the fire you must now choose a different route, Describe your new route.

3   An ambulance is also sent for. Describe the route it takes from the hospital. List the grid squares the ambulance passes through.

One step further

1   Imagine you are the child trapped by the fire.

Describe how the fire started.

2   Write a story with the title 'Trapped by fire'.

3   Fires can start in many ways. Make a list of all the ways you can think of. Talk to your parents and friends about this.

Assignment B

The pictures show what happens when an emergency call is received at the fire station.

Describe what each picture shows.

The water used to fight the fire comes from fire hydrants. Fire hydrants are marked by metal plates in the street. Make rubbings of the metal plates in your area.

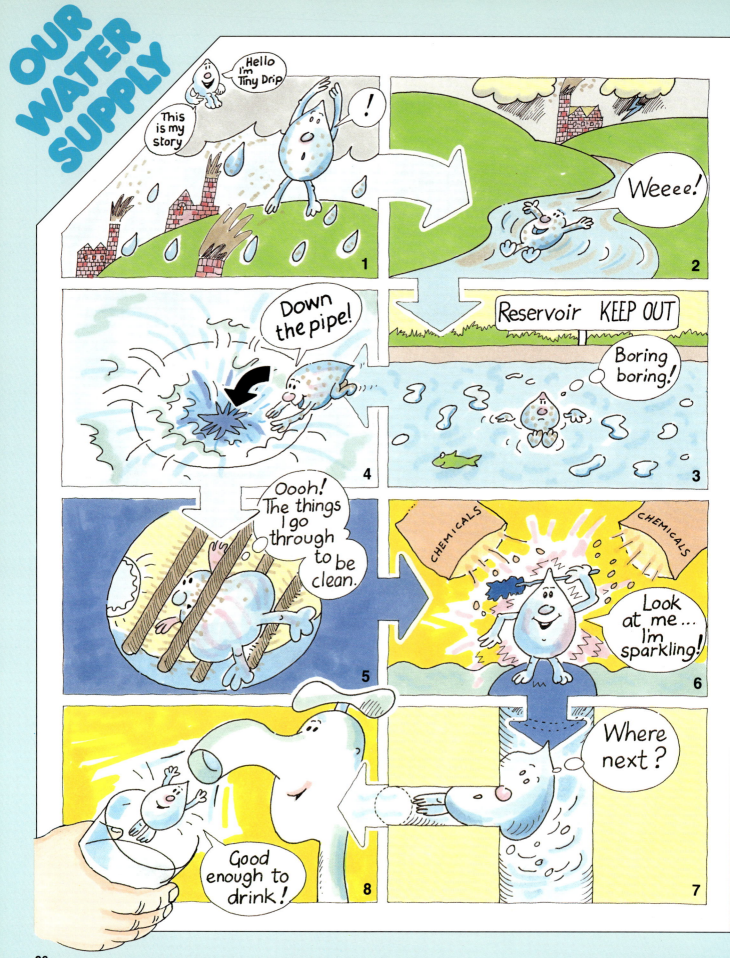

Assignment

Here are eight sentences about the journey of a drop of water.

They are not in the correct order.

Arrange the sentences so that they match the order of Tiny Drip's journey.

- The water from the stream collects in a large storage area - called a **reservoir**.
- When the tap is turned the water shoots out.
- When clouds cool they drop water onto the hills.
- Chemicals are added to make the water safe to drink.
- When the water is needed it leaves the reservoir through a large pipe.
- The water is pumped along main pipes and down narrow branch pipes to houses.
- The water passes through a narrow mesh which acts as a filter to remove most of the dirt.
- The rainwater collects in streams and runs downhill.

One step further

1 If an underground pipe is cracked what might happen to the colour of the water?

2 Imagine a pipe in your loft bursts following some cold icy weather.

Describe what might happen in your home.

Find out how to turn off the water supply to your home.

3 Poor old Tiny Drip looks as though he will soon be swallowed, but perhaps not. Carry on the story of Tiny's journey.

This picture shows what reservoirs, treatment centres and pipes look like.

If you write to your local water authority they will send you information about how water reaches your town.

DIRTY WATER

This is a picture of Dr John Snow. He worked in a small area of London called Soho. On August 30th, 1854 a terrible disease called Cholera struck. By September 8th five hundred people had died in Soho. No one knew how people caught cholera. Dr Snow had an idea that it was because people drank dirty water. He drew a map putting a black dot where each victim lived. He also marked on his map where each water pump stood.

Dr Snow's map of cholera deaths in Soho, London, 1854.

KEY

 Deaths from cholera

Pumps A to K

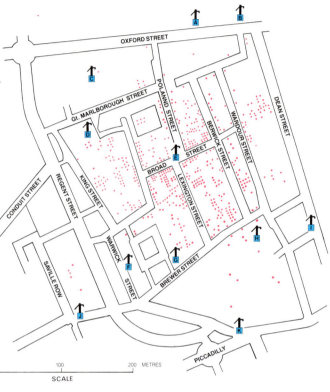

Assignment A

1 How many pumps were there in Soho in 1854?

2 Where were the most of the deaths? (Look at the map.)

3 Which water pump do you think was the one with the dirtiest water?

Dr Snow made the authorities take away the pump in Broad Street on September 8th. There were no more cholera deaths. The disease was carried in dirty water. Soho streets were full of rubbish and the rain washed this filth into the ground where the pump water came from.

One step further A

1 Write what you think it was like to be a child in Soho in August 1854. Here are some words to help:

old houses packed together, dark alleys, piles of rotting manure from animals and humans, filthy rubbish in streets, terrible smells, fear, death.

2 Look up cholera in your school encyclopedia.

Contact your local health centre or nurse. Find out where in the world cholera still exists today.

Do you know that your family pays the local water company to make sure that the water in our taps is clean?

The map shows how water from the river Thames is used. People in London may drink water that has been used several times before!

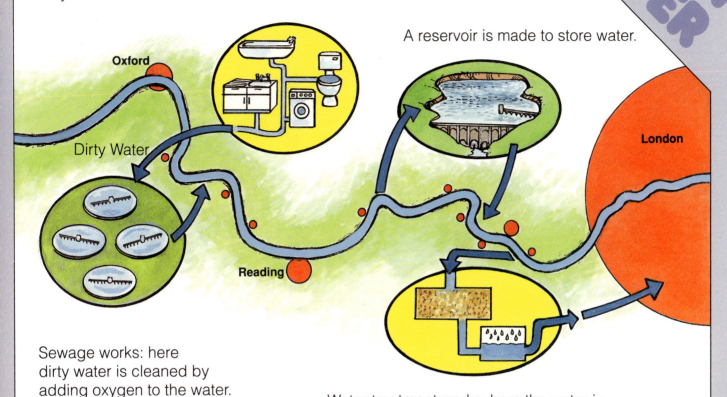

Oxford

Dirty Water

A reservoir is made to store water.

London

Reading

Sewage works: here dirty water is cleaned by adding oxygen to the water.

KEY

 Town

Water treatment works: here the water is passed through sand to make it cleaner. Chemicals are added to make it completely safe to drink.

Assignment B

Look at the map and diagrams.

1. Name three places in the house where dirty water comes from.

2. Where does the dirty water go when it leaves the house?

3. What is a reservoir?

4. How is the water purified at the water treatment works?

5. How many towns on the Thames Valley map use the same water over and over again?

One step further B

1. What would happen in London if the drinking water was not made clean?

2. Find out how much money your water charge is for one year.

3. Find out where your town's water supply comes from?

4. Where is your nearest sewage works?

Did you know?

Did you know that it is best to use white toilet paper? The dye in coloured paper is difficult to get rid of at the sewage works.

A VILLAGE WITHOUT CLEAN WATER

Doctor Snow improved the health of the people of London by proving that dirty water can cause disease. Nowadays in Britain we take it for granted that when we turn on a tap we shall have clean water.

In many parts of the world people are still without clean water. This village in India has no taps in the houses. The only water supply for the people is a pond.

DANGERS FROM DIRTY WATER

Sickness	Caused by
Cholera; Polio; Typhoid; Diarrhoea	Drinking dirty water. Washing hands, food or dishes in dirty water.
Malaria	Being bitten by mosquitoes which breed and bite near dirty water.
Leprosy; Worms	Bathing in dirty water. Germs enter the body through the mouth and skin.

Assignment A

Look at the picture and the chart:

1 How do you know the water is not clean?

2 What are the villagers doing that is dangerous to their health?

3 One woman is collecting drinking water. Which diseases might her family catch?

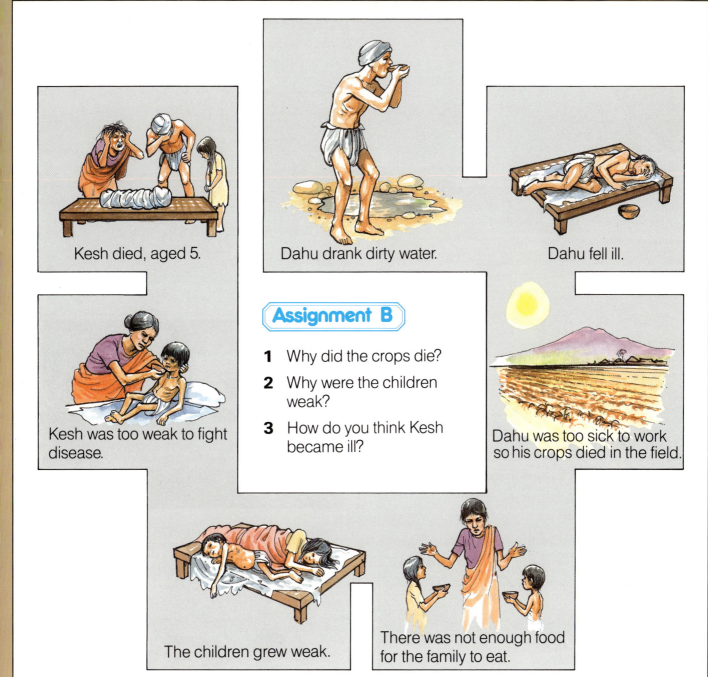

Kesh died, aged 5.

Dahu drank dirty water.

Dahu fell ill.

Assignment B

Kesh was too weak to fight disease.

1 Why did the crops die?

2 Why were the children weak?

3 How do you think Kesh became ill?

Dahu was too sick to work so his crops died in the field.

The children grew weak.

There was not enough food for the family to eat.

One step further

1 If you were Kesh's mother how would you feel?

Describe your feelings.

2 Imagine you were Dahu. You could see your family growing weak but you were not strong enough to work.

How would you feel?

3 If Dahu had drunk clean water all the other events might have been different.

Draw a 7 picture story of what might have happened.

4 What do the poor people of this village need if they are to be healthy and fit for work?

A WELL FOR THE VILLAGE

The Indian government wanted to help the villagers by providing a supply of clean water.

Experts checked if there was clean underground water near the village.

A **tube well** was driven through the ground to the water below. Local people did the work.

A handpump was fitted to the top of the tube well.
Villagers can now pump up clean water.

A local man was trained to look after the pump.
He can do simple repairs and makes sure that the water is always pure.

Assignment A

1 Why is the underground water cleaner than the pond water?

2 Why is it important that a local man should know how to repair the pump?

3 What should the 'pump man' do if he finds the water being pumped up is no longer pure?

4 Imagine you have to collect all your water from a well. How would this change life at home?

The new water supply has made the villagers much healthier.
It has changed their lives in other ways.

Here is a map of the village.

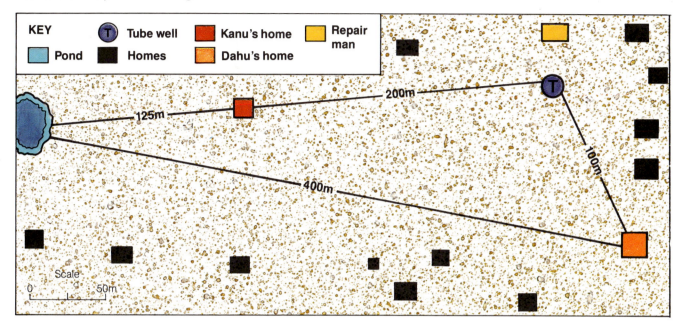

Assignment B

1 How far from the pond does Dahu live?

2 How far from the tube well does he live?

3 How much further from his house is the pond than the tube well?

4 Which is nearer to Kanu's home, the pond or the tube well?

5 If you were Kanu's wife where would you go for your water, the pond or the tube well?

6 Why do you think the pump repair man lives where he does?

One step further

Dahu's wife can carry 10 litres of water (she calls it 'Pani') in one journey.

Her family uses 80 litres in the home every day.

1 How many journeys a day must she make?

2 Each journey takes ten minutes. How long does she spend each day carrying water?

Do you think it is easy for Dahu's wife to carry 10 litres of water 100 m? Now you can find out for yourselves.

Pour ten litres of water into buckets.

Carry the buckets of water for 100 m.

Put the results for your class in a chart.

NAME	NUMBER OF RESTS	TIME TAKEN OVER 100M	AMOUNT SPILT

3 How many children spilled water?

4 How many needed a rest?

5 What was the quickest time?

6 What was the slowest time?

7 You probably use 170 litres of water a day. How long would it take you to carry this from a well?

WATER IN THE HOME

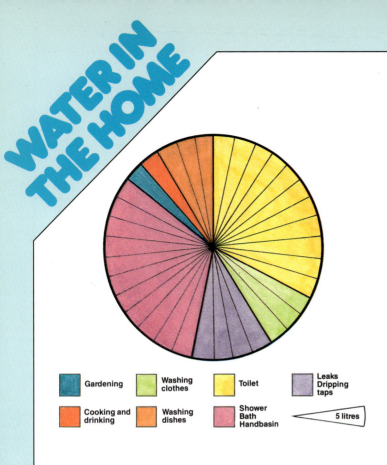

Gardening

Cooking and drinking

Washing clothes

Washing dishes

Toilet

Shower Bath Handbasin

Leaks Dripping taps

5 litres

Every day each person in Britain uses an average of 170 litres of water in the home. The pie chart shows how we use this water.

Assignment A

1 Which uses more water, washing dishes, cooking or drinking?

2 Does gardening take more or less water than the toilet?

3 Is more water used in the bathroom or the kitchen?

4 Which of the uses of water is really a waste of water?

5 How many litres of water are used on the garden?

People in other countries use different amounts of water.

The block graph shows how much water people in six other countries use in the home.

Number of litres used each day

USA   INDIA   SWEDEN   MEXICO   USSR   AFGHANISTAN

Assignment B

1 In which country do people use the most water?

2 In which countries do people use more water than in Britain?

3 How many litres are used each day in Sweden?

4 In which two countries do people use the same amount of water?

One step further

1 Use an atlas to find Britain and the six countries in the graph.

2 North Americans use more water than British people. What do they use the extra water for?

In dry summers parts of Britain can be short of water. When there is a drought people are not allowed to wash their cars or water their gardens. If the drought is really bad, water to houses can be turned off. Special taps called stand-pipes are put in the street and people queue for water.

FACTS ABOUT WATER

A flush of the toilet	10 litres
Brushing your teeth for 1 minute	15 litres
Automatic washing machine	140 litres
Taking a bath	120 litres
Taking a shower	10 litres
Using a garden hose for 1 hour	900 litres

Assignment C

1 Brushing your teeth while the tap is running uses a great deal of water. Can you think of ways of using less?

2 Look at the pairs of pictures above. Which method from each pair uses least water to do the job?

3 Draw three pictures of your own showing other ways of saving water.

A reservoir during a drought

35

RAIN

Doctor Foster went to Gloucester in a shower of rain. He stepped in a puddle right up to his middle and never went there again.

If Doctor Foster had known how to measure rainfall he would never have set off in the first place!

Mr Soak is as happy as can be. Postwoman Penny Black is miserable. They feel like this because it is raining.

Assignment A

Look at the pictures and chart.

1 Why do you think Mr Soak is pleased?

2 Why do you think Penny Black is sad?

3 If it were a sunny day how do you think Penny and Mr Soak would feel?

4 What was the weather like on Friday?

5 On which two days did it rain?

6 On which days do you think Mr Soak was happy?

7 How do you think Penny Black felt on Friday?

Sajid has made this record of the weather for the school week.

Monday	Tuesday	Wednesday	Thursday	Friday
sun	rain	sun and cloud	rain	sun

When we measure rainfall we include these four types.

rain   **sleet**   **snow**   **hail**

Sajid.. on which day did the MOST rain fall?

I don't know – I only made a record of whether it rained --- NOT how much!

Rain collects in a container called a rain gauge.

Once a day Sajid empties the water into a measuring cylinder.

He records the amount of rain on a chart.

This is Sajid's chart for one week at school.

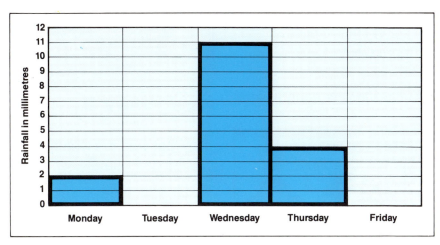

Assignment B

1 Which day had the heaviest rainfall?

2 Which two days were dry?

3 How much rain fell altogether during the school week?

4 Use Sajid's record of rainfall to draw a weather symbol chart for five days.

Different towns have different amounts of rain. The chart shows one day's rain for six towns.

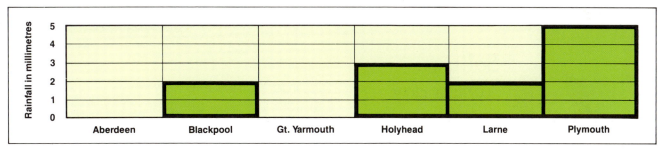

Assignment C

1 Which was the wettest town?

2 In which towns would you have needed an umbrella?

3 Who would be busier in Blackpool, the deckchair attendant or the arcade attendant?

One step further

Some newspapers show the amount of daily rainfall for major towns. Collect these figures for a week and record them on a chart.

1 Make a league table with the wettest town at the top, the driest at the bottom.

2 Use an atlas to draw a map showing where the towns are.

Mr Crock is unhappy. Miss Cone is delighted. They both feel this way because today it is hot.

Assignment A

1 Why do you think Mr Crock is sad?

2 Why do you think Miss Cone is happy?

3 If the day was cold, how do you think each of them would feel?

Sally has made this record of the weather for the school week.

Assignment B

Monday	Tuesday	Wednesday	Thursday	Friday
☀️	☁️	☀️	⛅	🌧️
sun	cloud	sun	sun and cloud	rain

1 What was the weather like on Friday?

2 On which days was it sunny all day?

3 Which day was sunny for a part of the day?

4 On which days would Mr Crock have been happy?

Sally.... which day was the hottest?

I don't know.... I only made a record of whether the sun shone.. NOT how HOT it was!

In order to measure how hot or cold it is Sally needs to use a **thermometer**. A thermometer has a glass tube.

Inside the tube there is mercury or alcohol. When it warms up it **expands** and rises up the tube. When it cools it will fall back down the tube. The numbers on the side of the thermometer show how hot or cold it is – they show the **temperature**.

This is Sally's temperature chart for one week at school.

She measured the temperature outside in the shade, at noon each day.

Assignment C

1 Which days of the week had the same temperature?

2 Which was the hottest day?

3 How much hotter was Tuesday than Thursday?

4 On which day would Miss Cone have been happiest?

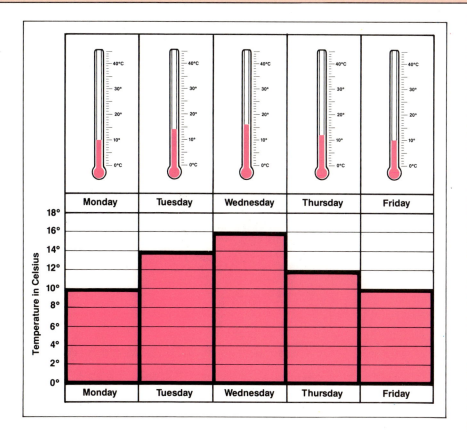

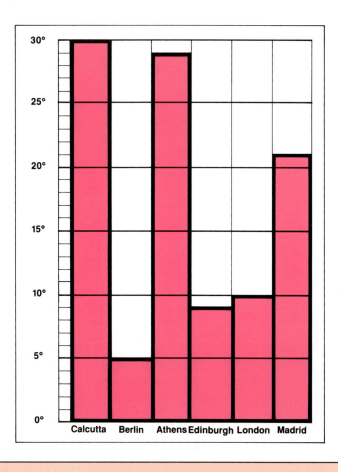

Assignment D

Sally looked in the daily paper and found the temperatures for these six cities around the world.

1 Which city had the highest temperature?

2 How much hotter was London than Berlin?

3 Which of the two British cities was warmer?

One step further

1 On an outline map of the world mark on the six cities shown in Sally's graph. Use an atlas to help you.

2 Use a national newspaper to collect temperature figures for different cities. Make a league table with the hottest at the top and the coldest at the bottom.

THE DAIRY FARM

This is George Hay's dairy farm in Devon.
To see what is going on in each building the artist has left the roofs off.
The cows live indoors at this time of year and are fed on silage.
Silage is grass which was cut in the summer, put in a heap, squashed and covered by plastic sheeting. It has a strong smell and cows love it.

KEY

1	Farmhouse	5	Silage	8	Pig unit	12	Garden
2	Machinery store	6	Straw	9	Cows' collecting yard	13	Road
3	Milking parlour	7	Cows in calf	10	Farmyard	14	Rubbish tip
4	Covered yard for cows		and calves	11	Manure		

Assignment A

1 Which season of the year is it?
   Give reasons to explain your choice.

2 Which animal is most important on a dairy farm?

3 List the other animals on Mr Hay's farm.

4 Which animal is tough enough to live out in the fields at this time of year?

5 How does it keep out the cold?

One step further

1 Design and make a model of a farm.

2 Design buildings with roofs you can remove.

3 Draw a map of the farm. An easy way is to stand on a chair and look down on your model. Draw what you see. This will be a map of the farm. Put labels on your map.

This is a picture of the same dairy farm ten years later. William Hay, George's son, is now in charge of the farm. Will is keen on **conservation**. This means he wants to make the farm better for wildlife (plants and animals), and more interesting for people.

Assignment B

1   Which season of the year is it? How can you tell?

2   Which animals are in the fields?

3   William has made the farm better for wildlife and people in places A, B, C, D and E. Fill in the table.

4   What other changes have happened?

5   What other changes to the farm could help William make money?

CHANGE MADE BY WILLIAM	WHY IS IT BETTER?	WHAT OR WHO WILL BENEFIT?
A		
B		
C		
D		
E		

A DAIRY FARMER'S DAY

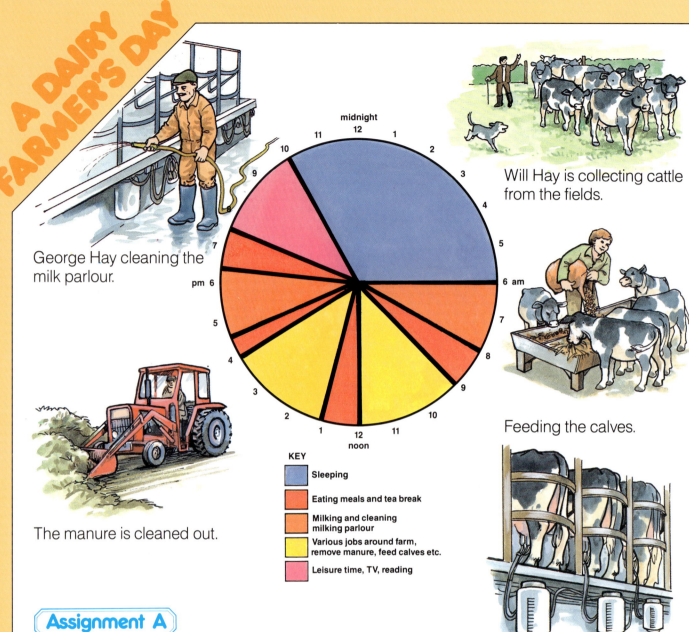

George Hay cleaning the milk parlour.

The manure is cleaned out.

Will Hay is collecting cattle from the fields.

Feeding the calves.

KEY

- Sleeping
- Eating meals and tea break
- Milking and cleaning milking parlour
- Various jobs around farm, remove manure, feed calves etc.
- Leisure time, TV, reading

A record of how much milk each cow gives is kept.

Assignment A

1. What time does the farmer get out of bed?

2. How many hours does he work in one day?

3. How many times a day are the cows milked?

4. Why has the milking parlour to be kept spotlessly clean?

5. Which job would you enjoy most?

6. Why is it difficult for a dairy farmer to go away on holiday?

7. What happens if he is ill?

One step further A

1. Mr Hay's cows are black and white.

   Find out in the school library which breed of cow this is.

2. Each cow produces about 20 litres of milk a day in summer. How much milk is produced by one cow in a week?

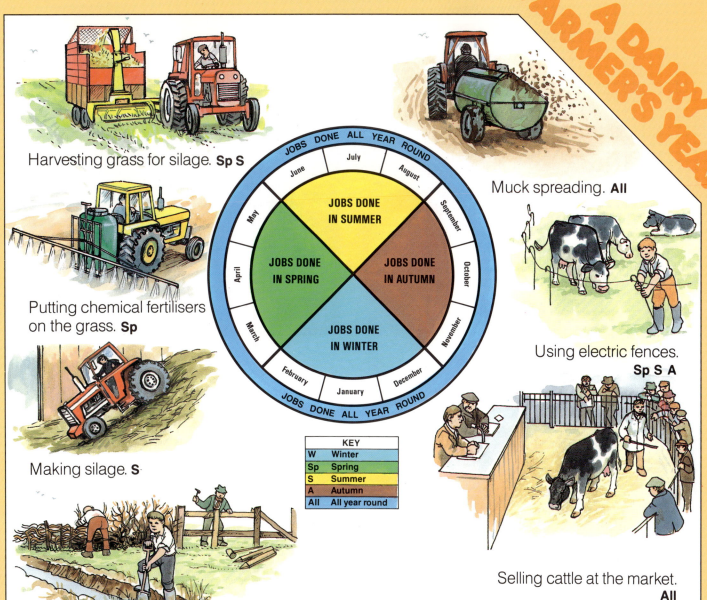

Harvesting grass for silage. **Sp S**

Putting chemical fertilisers on the grass. **Sp**

Making silage. **S**

Muck spreading. **All**

Using electric fences. **Sp S A**

Selling cattle at the market. **All**

Cutting hedges, mending fences, digging ditches. **W Sp**

JOBS DONE ALL YEAR ROUND

June · July · August · May · September · April · October · March · November · February · January · December

JOBS DONE IN SUMMER

JOBS DONE IN SPRING

JOBS DONE IN AUTUMN

JOBS DONE IN WINTER

JOBS DONE ALL YEAR ROUND

KEY	
W	Winter
Sp	Spring
S	Summer
A	Autumn
All	All year round

Assignment B

1 Make a list of the jobs done each season on the farm.

2 When is the best time of year for the farmer to have a holiday?

3 Why does the farmer use an electric fence?

One step further B

Britain belongs to a group of countries called the European Community (or E.C.).
The E.C. produces more milk, butter and cheese than is needed. Discuss with your friends what should be done about this. Here are some ideas:

a) Reduce the number of cows on each dairy farm.

b) Pay the farmers less for milk, butter and cheese.

c) Give the surplus dairy produce to starving people.

MILK

Neil Gregson collects milk from 10 farms each day. He starts at 8 a.m. and returns to the dairy by 2 p.m. The milk is put into large refrigerated stainless steel containers to keep it cool and fresh.

At the dairy the milk is **pasteurised**.

This means the milk is heated until all germs are killed.

It is then cooled to keep it fresh.

Jill Rodgers delivers 700 bottles of milk to 500 houses everyday. This is her day's work:

3 a.m.	–	gets out of bed
4 a.m.	–	arrives at dairy
4.30 a.m.	–	starts milk round
8.30 – 9 a.m.	–	breakfast
1.30 p.m.	–	finishes milk round

Assignment A

1 How many farms does Neil Gregson collect milk from each day?

2 How many hours does it take him?

3 What does pasteurising mean?

4 What is happening to the milk in the photograph?

5 How many houses does Jill Rodgers deliver milk to?

6 How many hours does it take her to do her round?

One step further A

Conduct a milk survey of your class.

The chart shows you what to find out.

	NUMBER OF PUPILS	HOW MUCH MILK DAILY	PRICE PAID
Have milk delivered			
Milk from shops			

1 Where do most people get their milk from?

2 Who sells the cheapest milk?

3 More and more people are buying milk from supermarkets. How will this affect Jill?

4 What are the advantages and disadvantages of using powdered milk?

Milk can be made into cheese, butter and yoghurt.
These are all **dairy** products.

Where does our cheese come from?

Camembert

Brie

Port Salut

Roquefort
(ewe's milk cheese)

Eire

United Kingdom

Denmark

Netherlands

Germany

France

Switzerland

Italy

Spain

Danish Blue

Edam

Gouda

Emmental

Mozzarella
(buffalo's milk cheese)

1 Name three cheeses from the north of France.

2 Which cheese with a red coat comes from the Netherlands?

3 Which is the buffalo milk cheese and where does it come from?

4 Which cheese has large holes and which two countries does it come from?

5 Name two cheeses with blue veins. Where do they come from?

One step further B

1 Name three animals whose milk is made into cheese.

2 List five British cheeses named after places.

3 Find these places in an atlas.

4 Draw graphs to show the favourite cheeses of a) your family b) your class

45

Sajid and Farah were surprised to see a Dutch girl in their local supermarket. They knew she was Dutch because of the clothes and clogs she wore. Her job was to visit supermarkets and give away samples of Dutch cheese.

Rita told Farah that she only wears clogs when she is working in Britain. At home in the Netherlands young people wear the same kind of clothes as people in Britain.

Tourists to the Netherlands like to see old-fashioned scenes. We call them **traditions**. There is a famous cheese market at Alkmaar where the workers wear traditional clothes and carry the cheeses in a special way.

Dutch Edam Cheese only has a red wax covering when it is sold in Britain. It is a tradition which helps to sell the cheese. In the Netherlands Edam is yellow on the outside.

Assignment A

1 What differences do you see between the people at Alkmaar and the people in an ordinary street in the Netherlands?

2 Look at this street in the Netherlands. Make a list of things which are the same as streets in Britain.

3 Now list the differences.

A street in the Netherlands

Rashid is an Arab businessman.

He works in an office.

He goes home at 5 o'clock.

How do you think he travels?

Sueyfong lives in Hong Kong.

She works in a factory making televisions.

Which is Sueyfong's home?

T.V. adverts do not always show real-life situations. They often show stereotypes.

Assignment B

1 What would your parent say if you came home like Sam?

2 Who washes the clothes in your family?

3 Do T.V. adverts show men or women doing the washing?

One step further

Our ideas of what other people are like are called **stereotypes**. What do you think Eskimos, North American Indians and people from France are like?

Find out if your ideas are true.

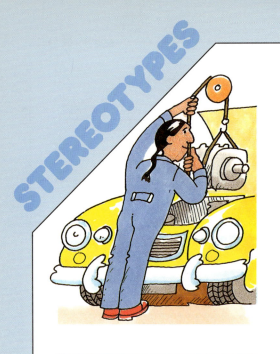

Bill is a North American Indian. He works in a garage as a mechanic.

When he needs food for the family where does he go?

Glenys is a typist. She works in Cardiff, Wales.

She goes dancing twice a week.

How does she dress for a disco?

Rajid is an Airline pilot. He lives in Delhi, India.

When he is tired which type of bed do you think he sleeps on?

Eric lives in Alaska, U.S.A. He is an Inuit. (In the olden days Inuits were called Eskimos.) Eric works for an oil company. Which is his house?

Jane works on a farm in Devon, England. When she leaves the farm to go home what do you think she looks like?

Assignment

1 Look at picture B. Some people, who have never been to England, think that all Englishmen wear bowler hats and carry briefcases. People who live in England know this is not true. We call this kind of false picture a **stereotype**.

A   B   C   D

Here are four stereotypes of an Englishman, Welshman, Scotsman and Irishman.

Complete the chart.

STEREOTYPE	PICTURE	COUNTRY	EMBLEM
Englishman	B	England	
Welshman			
Scotsman			
Irishman			

2 Do you think the people of Britain are really like these stereotypes?

Draw pictures to show what they are really like.

Compare your picture with the stereotype.

INTO EUROPE

This map shows the whole of Europe. Some countries belong to the European Community (E.C.). These are shown in red print. The E.C. is growing, many countries wish to join. Perhaps one day the whole of Europe will be part of it. Russia and Turkey are partly in Europe and partly in Asia.

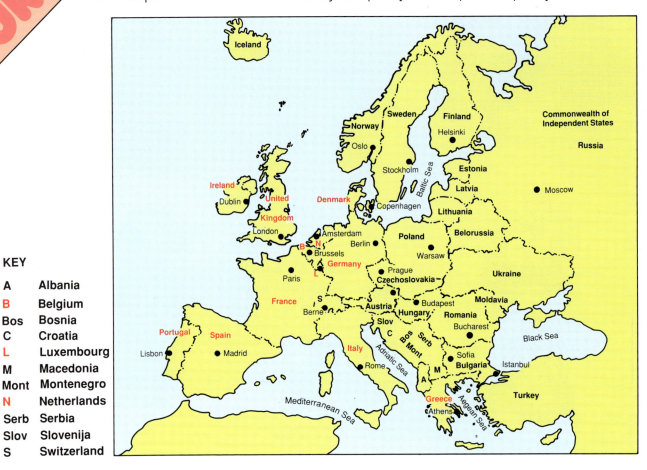

KEY

A	Albania
B	Belgium
Bos	Bosnia
C	Croatia
L	Luxembourg
M	Macedonia
Mont	Montenegro
N	Netherlands
Serb	Serbia
Slov	Slovenija
S	Switzerland

Assignment A

1 Name the capital cities of:
   a) Spain b) Italy c) Russia d) Norway

2 Which countries have these capital cities:
   a) Berlin b) Lisbon c) Paris d) Athens?

3 Starting from London each time, in which direction would you travel to visit:
   a) Berlin b) Paris c) Helsinki d) Rome?

4 Which sea is between
   a) U.K. and Denmark
   b) Greece and Turkey?

One step further A

1 If you travelled in a straight line from London which countries would you cross on your way to:
   a) Lisbon b) Berlin c) Budapest d) Sofia?

2 Complete the route chart.

FROM	TO	DIRECTION
London	Paris	South
Paris	Madrid	
Madrid	Rome	
Rome	Berlin	
Berlin	London	

For hundreds of years people have dreamed of linking England and France by a tunnel. The remains of a tunnel bored in 1880 can still be seen today.

The Channel Tunnel, finished in 1993, carries trains in both directions

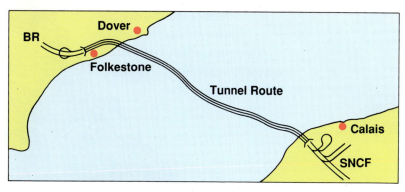

The Channel Tunnel was bored by gigantic boring machines which moved approximately 160 metres a week.

If we could see the Tunnel from the side it would look like this.

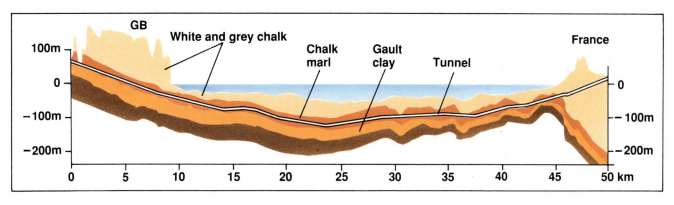

Assignment B

1 How wide is the English Channel?
2 How long is the Tunnel?
3 How deep is the water at its deepest?
4 How deep is the Tunnel at its deepest?

One step further B

1 Which type of rock does the Tunnel run through?
2 List the good and bad points of travelling through the Channel Tunnel.

TRAVEL IN EUROPE

Apart from the Channel Tunnel there are many other ways to travel from Britain to the rest of Europe.

The map shows some ferry and air routes linking Britain and Continental Europe.

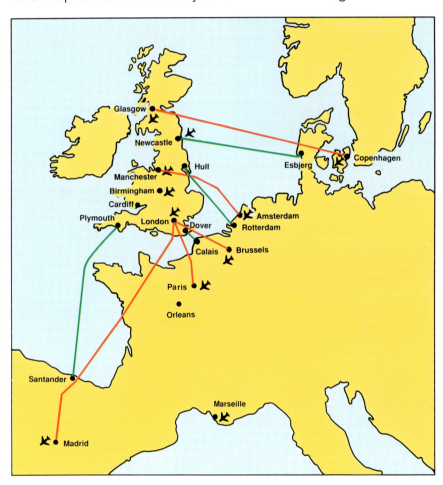

KEY

—— Flight paths

—— Ferry routes

✈ Airport

Assignment A

1 List the airports in England shown on the map.

2 Name the airport shown on the map in:
a) Scotland   b) Denmark
c) Belgium   d) Spain

3 Which is the shortest ferry route between Britain and the continent? Which is the longest?

One step further A

1 There are many other airports in Britain. Which is the nearest to you?

2 Carry out a class survey. Record the results on a chart like this:

EUROPEAN TRAVEL			
Name	From	To	By
Pat	Manchester	Brussels	plane
Walter	Birmingham	Blackpool	car

People travel for different reasons. They also have to think about distance, time and cost. Travel by plane is quick but you cannot take your car.

A — I live in Cardiff and need to visit Brussels on business for the day.

B — It's our wedding anniversary and we are flying to Amsterdam for the weekend. We live in Manchester.

C — We're taking the car to northern Spain for a camping holiday. We live in Glasgow.

D — I'm driving this load from London to Marseille.

E — I'm going to hike around Denmark for three weeks. I live near Newcastle.

Assignment B

Copy and complete the chart.

TRAVELLER	FROM	TO	BY
A	Cardiff	Brussels	train, plane
B			
C			
D			
E			

One step further B

1 Why did person D not fly from London to Marseille?

2 Why did persons B not drive and use the ferry?

3 Why did family C take the car instead of flying?

4 Make a list of reasons why people travel.

Sally is outdoors pouring water from a watering can onto a heap of sand.

1 Describe what is happening to the heap of sand.

2 Draw the pattern you can see made by the water on the sand.

3 Put these labels on your drawing:
a) water falling   b) sand washing away
c) sand collecting.

One step further A

Try out Sally's experiment. First use a heap of sand and then a heap of sand with large and small stones in it.

What differences do you see?

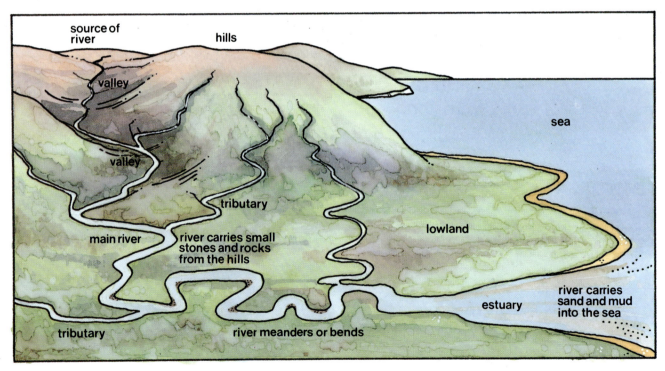

Where a river begins is called its **source**. Many rivers have their sources in hills because more rain falls over highland than over lowland. Rivers wear away the ground to make valleys. This wearing away of soils and rocks is called **erosion**. Most rivers flow into the sea. The wide point where the river meets the sea is called the **river mouth** or **estuary**.

The map shows the three longest rivers in England and Wales.

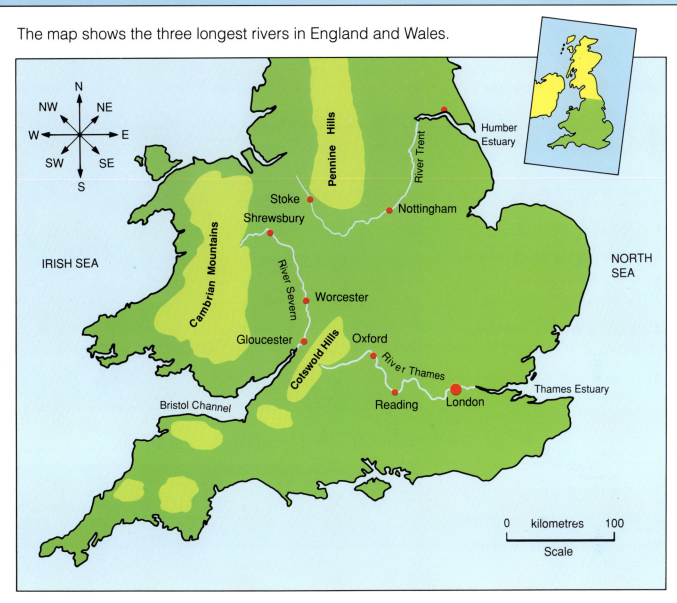

KEY ◼ High land ◼ Low land

Assignment B

1 Name the three rivers.

2 Which river has its source in Wales?

3 Which flows through London?

4 Use a piece of string to find which river is the longest?

5 Which river is furthest north?

6 Which river is furthest west?

7 Name two towns each river passes through.

One step further B

Copy and complete the chart

RIVER	HIGH LAND SOURCE	ESTUARY	SEA IT JOINS
Severn			
Thames			
Trent			

RIVER TRENT

The river in Dovedale, Derbyside.

Assignment A

1 Describe the land.

2 Is the river wide or narrow?

3 Is the river near its source or its mouth?

4 Is this a town or country area?

5 What is growing on the valley sides?

The river passing under the Humber Bridge.

Assignment B

1 Describe the land.

2 Is the river wide or narrow?

3 Is it near its source or its mouth?

4 Is this a town or country area?

5 Is it a road or rail bridge?

One step further A

1 Use an atlas to find the name of your nearest river.

2 Where is its source?

3 Where does it enter the sea?

4 Where is the nearest river bridge to you?

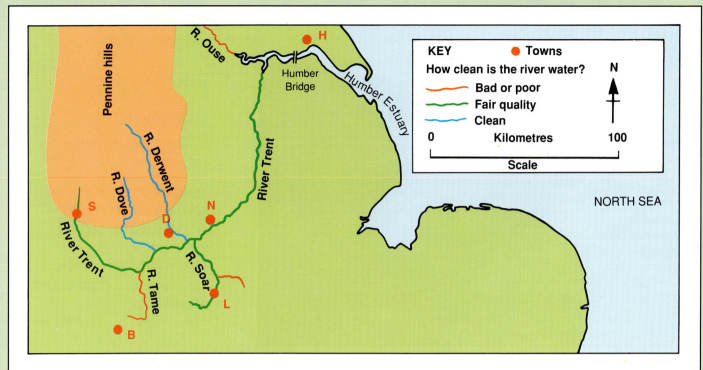

Tributaries are rivers which flow into the main river.

Assignment C

1 Name two clean tributaries of the River Trent.

2 Name a polluted tributary.

3 Name three tributaries which have their sources in the Pennines.

4 Name one tributary which flows north and one which flows south.

One step further B

1 Use your atlas to find the names of the six towns on the map.

2 Which tributaries are likely to have the most fish?

3 How might these people pollute a river?
a) a farmer b) a factory owner
c) a school child?

Look at the photograph.

4 What are the people doing?

5 What have they collected?

6 Design a river code which will help prevent pollution. Work as a team and design a poster to get your message across.

RIVERS IN FLOOD

Assignment A

1 Describe what has happened in the photograph.

2 How do you think the people feel?

3 Imagine there is a flood. How would you try to stop the water getting into your home?
What would happen to the carpets, furniture and other items?

If it rains very hard and rivers cannot carry all of the water they overflow. This is called a **flood**.

Assignment B

The graph shows a week's rainfall at Dampton. Look at the depth of water in the section of the River Damp for each day of the week.

Copy and fill in this chart for the week.

Day	Rainfall in millimetres	Depth of river in metres	Tick days when river flooded the fields
Monday			
Tuesday			
Wednesday			
Thursday			
Friday			
Saturday			
Sunday			

What link can you see between rainfall and river level?

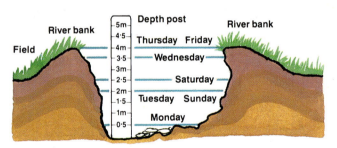

A cross section through the River Damp showing the depths of water for each day of the week

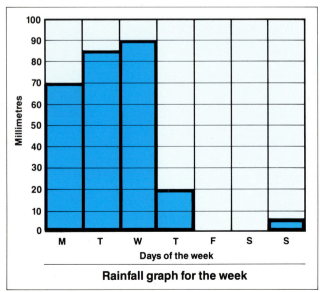

Rainfall graph for the week

Assignment C

1 Can you name each of the activities which take place on or near the river?

2 Which of the sports are mainly done
a) in summer b) in winter c) all the year?

3 Sports on or near rivers can be dangerous. What safety precautions are needed for each sport?

4 Conduct a survey to find out the most popular sports in your class. How many are to do with water?

One step further

1 If this river became polluted how would each sport be affected?

2 Would any be impossible?

3 Find out which activities take place on or near your local river.

Deserts have less than 250 mm of rain a year. In some years there may be no rain at all. During the day temperatures can reach 50°C in the hottest deserts. Nights can be bitterly cold.

The world's deserts

Stony and rocky deserts

Sandy deserts

Assignment A

1 Are most of the world's deserts sandy or stony?

2 Give three reasons why travelling across the desert can be dangerous.

3 Is a camel or a Landrover better for travelling across sand dune deserts?

One step further A

Imagine you are going on a seven day journey across a desert by Landrover. Make a list of the things you would take with you. Think about distance, temperatures, direction and dangers.

Deep beneath the desert rocks there is often water. Where this water rises to the surface the desert is changed. Plants grow, people and animals have water to drink. These places are called **oases**.

Assignment B

1 Describe the oasis in the photograph.

2 Why have houses been built at this oasis?

3 What might happen if the oasis dries up?

4 Why does the date palm have long roots?

5 List three uses a traveller on a camel could make of the date palm.

One step further B

1 Collect labels from date packets sold in your local shops. Find out where the dates came from and find the countries on a map.

2 Hot deserts are close to the tropics of Cancer and Capricorn.
Use the map on pages 62/63 to find the name of a hot desert in each of:
a) South America
b) North America
c) Africa
d) South West Asia.

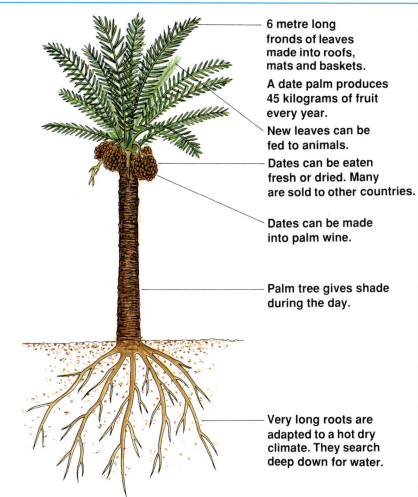

6 metre long fronds of leaves made into roofs, mats and baskets.

A date palm produces 45 kilograms of fruit every year.

New leaves can be fed to animals.

Dates can be eaten fresh or dried. Many are sold to other countries.

Dates can be made into palm wine.

Palm tree gives shade during the day.

Very long roots are adapted to a hot dry climate. They search deep down for water.

RAINFALL

ARCTIC OCE

Mainly light snowfalls

Norway

UK

EUROPE

The Alps

Mediterranean Sea

Sahara Desert

AFRICA

Nigeria

Congo

Zaire

Kalahari Desert

Alaska

Northern territories

Canada

British Columbia

NORTH AMERICA

United States

Californian Desert

ATLANTIC

Venezuela

Equator

Colombia

Amazon Forest

Brazil

OCEAN

PACIFIC

SOUTH AMERICA

Atacama Desert

③

OCEAN

Patagonia Desert

A

Mainly li

Wettest Places — in millimetres

AREA	GREATEST RAINFALL IN 24 HOURS	GREATEST RAINFALL IN ONE MONTH	GREATEST RAINFALL IN ONE YEAR
U.K.	Martinstown, Dorset 279 mm	Llyn Llydan Snowdon, Wales 1,436mm	Sprinkling Tarn, Cumbria 6,527 mm
U.S.A.	Alvin, Texas 1,092 mm	Kukui Maui, Hawaii 2,718 mm	Kukui Maui, Hawaii 14,681 mm
India	Cherrapunji 1,036 mm	Cherrapunji 9,299 mm	Cherrapunji 26,461 mm
World	La Reunion, an island in the Indian Ocean 1,870 mm	Cherrapunji 9,299 mm	Cherrapunji 26,461 mm

Driest Places — in millimetres

AREA	PLACE	AVERAGE RAINFALL IN ONE YEAR
U.K.	St. Osyth Marsh, Essex	513 mm
U.S.A.	Death Valley, California	41 mm
India	Shahjarh, Thar Desert	112 mm
World	Arica, Atacama desert, Chile.	0·7 mm

SIBERIA

PACIFIC

OCEAN

Gobi Desert

Japan

A S I A

China

Thar
Desert

SOUTH
EAST
ASIA

Desert

India

Philippines

Equator

Malaysia

Equator

New Guinea

INDIAN

OCEAN

Indonesia

AUSTRALASIA

Australian Desert

New Zealand

RCTIC OCEAN

ANTARCTICA

Assignment

Is

Complete this table.

	PLACE	COUNTRY	CONTINENT
Driest place in the world			
Wettest place in the world			

1 Measure and cut a piece of string 279 millimetres long. This is the depth of rainwater which fell at Martinstown in Dorset in 24 hours.

2 Measure and cut a piece of string 1,870 millimetres long.

This is the rain that fell in 24 hours at La Reunion.

Hang the pieces of string up in your classroom and label what each shows.

3 Look at the map of the world showing wet and dry places.

Can you name

- 2 deserts in Africa
- a very wet part of Europe
- a very dry part of South America
- a very wet forest.

THE WORLD ANNUAL RAINFALL

KEY

Very wet over

Over 1000mm

250mm - 1000mm

Very dry

Under 250mm

KEY   World's wettest places:

① = Cherrapunji

② = La Reunion

World's driest place:

③ = Arica, Chile

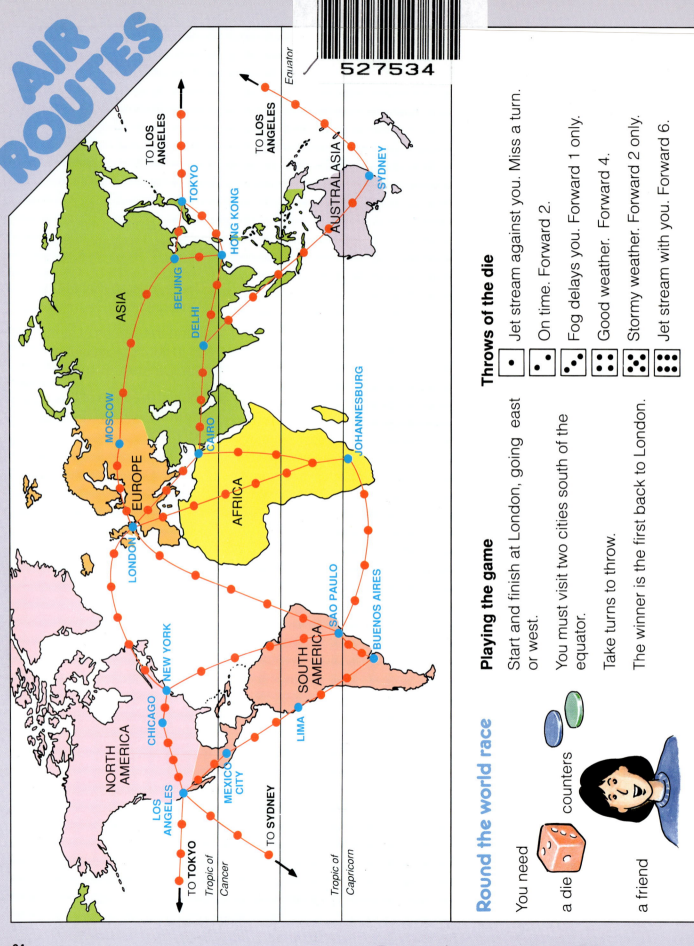

AIR ROUTES

527534

TO LOS ANGELES

TOKYO

Equator

TO LOS ANGELES

AUSTRALASIA

SYDNEY

HONG KONG

ASIA

BEIJING

DELHI

MOSCOW

CAIRO

EUROPE

AFRICA

JOHANNESBURG

LONDON

NORTH AMERICA

CHICAGO

NEW YORK

SAO PAULO

BUENOS AIRES

SOUTH AMERICA

LIMA

MEXICO CITY

LOS ANGELES

TO SYDNEY

Tropic of Cancer

Tropic of Capricorn

TO TOKYO

Throws of the die

- Jet stream against you. Miss a turn.
- On time. Forward 2.
- Fog delays you. Forward 1 only.
- Good weather. Forward 4.
- Stormy weather. Forward 2 only.
- Jet stream with you. Forward 6.

Playing the game

Start and finish at London, going east or west.

You must visit two cities south of the equator.

Take turns to throw.

The winner is the first back to London.

Round the world race

You need

a die   counters

a friend

64

5.25   2/01